The Summer

Lloyd Kajikawa

Illustrated by Mike Tofanelli

Contents

Rigby®

1 An Idea

Ayako and her mother moved into the Center Street apartment building three years ago, when they came to the United States from Japan. Since then, people from all over the world had moved into the building. Unfortunately, all of these people were so busy with their jobs and families that they didn't know each other very well. Mr. Vega—the building manager—thought this was a problem and brought it up at the weekly meeting of apartment neighbors.

"I think we should do something together so we can all get to know each other," he suggested.

Ayako looked around at all of the unfamiliar faces. Mr. Vega was right—she didn't really know anyone except her friend Adela. When she spotted Adela at the meeting, they smiled at each other. Ayako and Adela were best friends.

Mr. Vega asked if the group had any ideas.

"We could plant some flowers out front together," suggested one neighbor.

"Or we could all go to the movies together," said another.

"Or you could all come over to my apartment and help me clean out my closets," called out a third.

Everyone laughed at that, but no one really liked any of these ideas.

As Ayako listened, she began to think that a large party would be a good way to bring everyone together. She remembered how she had met Adela at a party at school. Maybe the building could have a party to celebrate the beginning of summer!

2 Ayako's Dream

Back at home, Ayako said, "Mom, I think we should have a party and invite all of the neighbors. A party is a very fun way to meet people!"

"You are so creative, Ayako-chan. But where would you have this party . . . here?" asked her mother, smiling.

That night Ayako dreamed that everyone in the building came to a huge party in her small, two-bedroom apartment. In her dream, everyone was having a great time and making new friends. The next morning, Ayako was so excited about her dream that she couldn't wait to tell Mr. Vega about her idea. Quickly she rushed down to the manager's office.

"Last night I dreamed that we had a wonderful building party in my apartment!" Ayako told Mr. Vega.

Mr. Vega smiled and gently said that everyone wouldn't fit in her apartment. Ayako told him that everyone *had* fit in her dream. Chuckling, Mr. Vega explained that there were 30 apartments in the building, with about 4 people in each.

Ayako multiplied the numbers together in her head and said, "That would be 120 people, and that *is* too many to fit in my apartment!"

"Yes, but I think that having a party is a great idea. Our community room holds 150 people, so we could have the party there," suggested Mr. Vega.

3 Making Plans

Ayako was thrilled that Mr. Vega liked her idea. Immediately she ran to find Adela because she knew they were a good team. Adela was good at planning and Ayako liked thinking up ideas.

"Adela, I talked to Mr. Vega about having a party for everyone in our apartment building, and he thought it was a great idea!" shouted Ayako.

"A party *is* a great idea!" Adela said. "Have you started planning yet?"

"No, that's why I was looking for you," replied Ayako. "Will you help me plan the party?"

"Yes, this is going to be so much fun!" Adela said, as the girls hurried to Ayako's apartment.

Adela said, "If the party is going to be in the community room, we'll need decorations!"

"We should have music and plenty of food for everyone, too!" Ayako exclaimed.

As the girls began to plan, they decided that hot dogs would be a good meal for the party.

"If there are 120 people, and each person eats 2 hot dogs," Adela explained, "then we'll need 240 hot dogs."

"Hot dogs come in packages of 10," Ayako's mother told them, and Adela quickly did some more math.

"If we divide 240 by 10, we get 24, so we'll need 24 packages of hot dogs," Adela announced.

"Don't forget that you will also need hot dog buns, drinks, napkins, and plates," Ayako's mother added.

"Wow, planning a party is a lot of work!" Ayako said, writing all of this down.

Our Party Plans

120 people × 2 hot dogs each = 240 hot dogs

240 hot dogs ÷ 10 hot dogs in a package = 24 packages

4 More Plans

Next Adela and Ayako decided that they should make a sign to tell people about the party and a map to tell people where the community room was.

Soon Ayako had made a sign and Adela had finished a map. "We really do make a good team," Adela said, taping her map to the bottom of Ayako's sign.

Just then Ayako's mother came into the room and said, "I've been thinking about your party. Do you have enough tables and chairs for everyone to be able to sit?"

Adela and Ayako looked at each other.

"Uh-oh," they said.

Meet Your Neighbors!
Celebrate the Beginning of Summer!
Come to the Building Party!
Day: Saturday
Time: 11:00 A.M. to 5:00 P.M.
Place: The Community Room

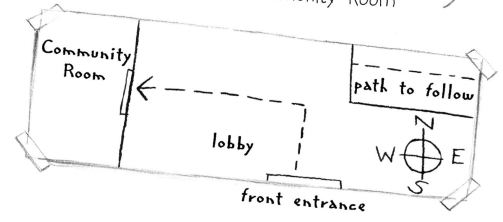

The girls found Mr. Vega and asked him to help them figure out how many tables and chairs they would need. Rolling out a large sheet of paper on his desk, he said, "This is a floor plan of the community room."

"We have 8 rectangular tables," Ayako counted.

"If we put 10 people at each table, then that takes care of 80 people, leaving 40 more since 120 minus 80 equals 40," Adela said. "Since 40 divided by 8 equals 5, we have to add 5 more chairs to each table. When we add those 5 chairs to the 10 that are already there, we'll have 15 chairs at each table."

Because the community room only had 100 chairs, and they needed 120, they decided to ask 20 people to bring extra chairs.

$$8 \text{ tables} \times 10 \text{ people per table} = 80 \text{ people}$$
$$120 \text{ people} - 80 \text{ people} = 40 \text{ people left}$$
$$40 \text{ people} \div 8 \text{ tables} = 5 \text{ people per table}$$

$$\begin{array}{r} 10 \text{ people per table} \\ + 5 \text{ people per table} \\ \hline 15 \text{ people per table} \end{array}$$

kitchen

counter

restroom | restroom

table | table | table

table | table | table

table | table

chairs →

5 Almost Everyone Is Happy

At the next weekly meeting, Mr. Vega told everyone that Ayako had come up with a great idea for getting everyone together. She was asked to come to the front, and for a moment, she felt very nervous about speaking. Then she thought about how important this party was and how it could help everyone get to know each other. Bravely she made herself stand up.

Scared at first, Ayako soon felt less afraid because everyone was smiling. She slowly explained all of the plans for the party: the food, the drinks, the music, everything. The more she talked about the party, the more excited she became. Soon she was so excited that she forgot to mention that Adela was helping her.

Adela sat sadly in the back of the room while Ayako and Mr. Vega passed around a chart so that the neighbors could sign up to bring things. After the meeting was over, Ayako noticed Adela and ran up to her.

Who?	What?	How many?	Needed When?
Ayako Kano	Cake	1	At the party
Mr. Lai	Extra table	1	The day before the party
Mrs. Domínguez	Hot dog buns	1 package	At the party
The Kim family	Chairs	4	The day before the party

"I think everyone likes our idea!" Ayako said happily.

"You mean they like *your* idea," Adela corrected Ayako. "You made it sound like you are the only one planning the party."

Surprised, Ayako explained that she had gotten so excited that she had just forgotten to mention Adela. Then she asked Adela to come help her plan decorations, certain that Adela would say yes. However, Adela said no and walked unhappily away.

6 A New Problem

The party was one day away, and Ayako really missed Adela. She told her mother the whole story and concluded, "I explained to her that I was so excited that I forgot to mention her."

"Ayako, you just need to figure out how to make things right with Adela," her mother told her.

Later that day, Mr. Vega invited both girls to help him decorate the community room. When they walked in, Ayako noticed for the first time how bare the room was—nothing but white walls, doors, and windows. There was no color except for the red "Exit" signs. Mr. Vega had lots of balloons and streamers, and he asked Ayako and Adela to help him figure out where to put them. Adela worked silently, still refusing to speak to Ayako.

23

Mr. Vega and Adela began to blow up the balloons while Ayako taped streamers to the tables. Ayako twirled the streamers so that they hung in paper curls around the table edges. Then Mr. Vega and Adela hung streamers from the ceiling in long, twisted arcs that decorated the empty room. In the center, Adela tied the arcs together, and Ayako added a group of red, blue, and yellow streamers that hung to the floor. Here and there, Adela taped green, purple, and white balloons to the streamers.

When they were finished, the plain community room had been transformed into a room of many colors, and it was ready for a party!

7 The Party

On the day of the party, some people were setting up chairs in the community room while others were busy laying out plates, hot dogs, chips, and other party supplies. One of the neighbors had brought his stereo and was now playing lively music while a few other people danced. Everyone was talking and laughing and having a good time.

Ayako entered the party carrying a chocolate cake that she and her mother had made together. It was Adela's favorite, and Ayako was hoping that the cake would help them become friends again.

Ayako decided to slice her cake so everyone could have a piece. She wanted to ask Adela for help dividing the cake into the right number of pieces, but Adela still was not speaking to her. Making a guess, Ayako sliced her cake so that it had 6 columns and 10 rows. However, before she could count the pieces, she saw Adela entering the room with her family. Adela walked away from Ayako, who stared sadly down at her cake.

"Ayako, I would love a piece of your delicious cake," Mrs. Vu said, holding out her plate. Ayako was about to hand Mrs. Vu a piece of cake when she realized that she had sliced her cake into 60 pieces—not 120! Ayako began to panic. Where was Adela when she needed her? Ayako looked across the room and saw Adela staring back at her.

8 Friends Again!

So embarrassed that she was about to cry, Ayako looked back at the cake and struggled to figure out what to do. However, the more she looked at the cake, the more confused and upset she became. Suddenly she heard Adela's voice.

"Please excuse us for a moment, Mrs. Vu, because we aren't quite finished cutting the cake," Adela said.

And with that, Adela took the cake server from Ayako's hand and made 12 columns where there had been 6 before. Therefore, they had twice as many pieces—120 pieces—enough for everyone to have one! Then Adela smiled at Ayako and carefully lifted a piece of the gooey chocolate cake onto Mrs. Vu's plate.

"Thanks, Adela," Ayako said as Mrs. Vu walked away.

The party was a success! Mr. Vega motioned for quiet and told everyone about the hard work that Ayako had done.

Before Ayako spoke, she ran over to Adela and whispered, "Come with me." Ayako led Adela to where Mr. Vega was standing and said, "Yes, I did a lot of work, but many people helped, especially my best friend, Adela!"

The room erupted with applause and cheers as the two girls smiled at each other—best friends again!